Contents

Dedications:

Thank you, to my Lord and Savior; for giving me the desire and skill-set to accomplish something to help guide others.

Thank you to my Wife, (Crystal Danyel); for the love, patients, and understanding while I spent a great amount of time and effort developing the content of this project.

Thank you to my Family (Pelmore's & Thorpe's); for all the lessons and support through the years of chasing my dreams

Thank you to the Company (Lincoln & Hill); for seeing this project as a viable asset to the mission & vision

Tags & Legend

Caution tag: depicts the subject or information should be approached carefully

Challenge tag: depicts individual or couple must complete an assignment

immediately before moving to next concept

Checkpoint tag: depicts location gauge during subject or individual progression

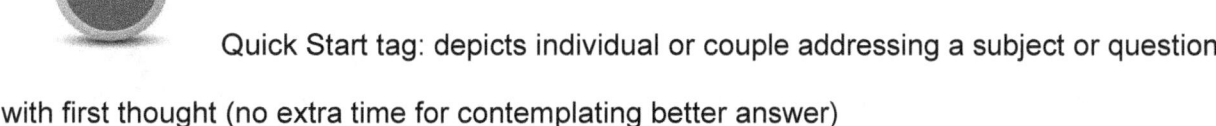

Discussion tag: depicts specific subject matter verbalized between male &

female

Quick Start tag: depicts individual or couple addressing a subject or question

with first thought (no extra time for contemplating better answer)

Reflection tag: depicts individuals thinking about subject or questions before providing an answer

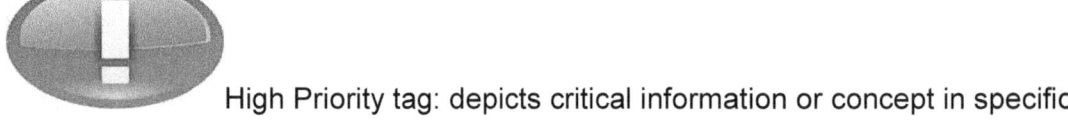

Practical Exercise tag: depicts individual or couple must complete an assignment before next session can proceed

Key Point tag: depicts main topics covered in specific chapters

High Priority tag: depicts critical information or concept in specific block

Advice tag: depicts information for emphasizing key point

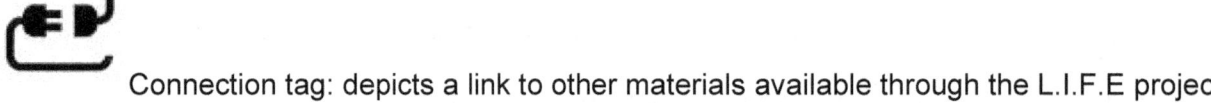

Connection tag: depicts a link to other materials available through the L.I.F.E project

Active Listening tag: depicts one individual should be actively listening each time another individual is talking in the communication process

Audio tag: depicts a piece of supplementary audio information

Video tag: depicts a piece of supplementary video information

Content Commentary tag: depicts supplementary data through public research & discussions that we may oppose or support but use for teaching

Definition tag: depicts word or phrase the is not considered common

Caveat tag: depicts a warning when considering information about this subject

Move Away tag: depicts a warning to move away from information, situation or person

Learn it tag: depicts information that is learned

Prerequisite tag: depicts information that must be introduced before learning a boarder concept

WB Block 1: *e21st* Century Introduction

The questions below reflect some of the most common areas of business concerns highlighted in this block. Answer all questions. **Discuss & Share** your answers with your cohort to provide in-depth understanding for each of your responses. Make additional notes if questions/concern aren't answered immediately, information provided in later blocks may also help you get clarification.

(Discussion Tag)

1.   As a business owner, do you understand the principles pertaining to the economic

system?

```

```

• (Quick Start Tag)

1.   Determine the typical positioning along the product adoption curve (innovator, early

adaptor, early majority, late majority, laggards) in an industry you relate too. Explain your

answer; did this information change your opinion of timing in business?

```

```

☺ (Reflection Point Tag)

1.   What does the Chasm mean to you? Be specific

| |
| |

☺ (Reflection Point Tag)

2.   What thinking method does your idea/product/company operate through? Be specific

---
| |
| |

◇ (Caution Tag)

1.   Which thinking method are you NOT leading your idea/product/company with along the adoption curve that you would be hesitant to attempt, whether it's short-term or long-term? Why?

| |
| |

◉ (Challenge Tag)

1.   Do you know any businesses in the position along the adoption curve that you would desire your company to be in? If so, what positive or negative characteristics do they have that influence you?

```
```

⁀ Block Key Points:

- All businesses & owners are not the same, however they must operate from a general category
- Characteristics or lack thereof that may deter you/your business from the optimal positioning.

⏳ Practical Exercise:

In each (5) categories list some businesses or people (to include how) you believe they fit into the category. Adoption Curve definitions are in Introduction Block of book for review.

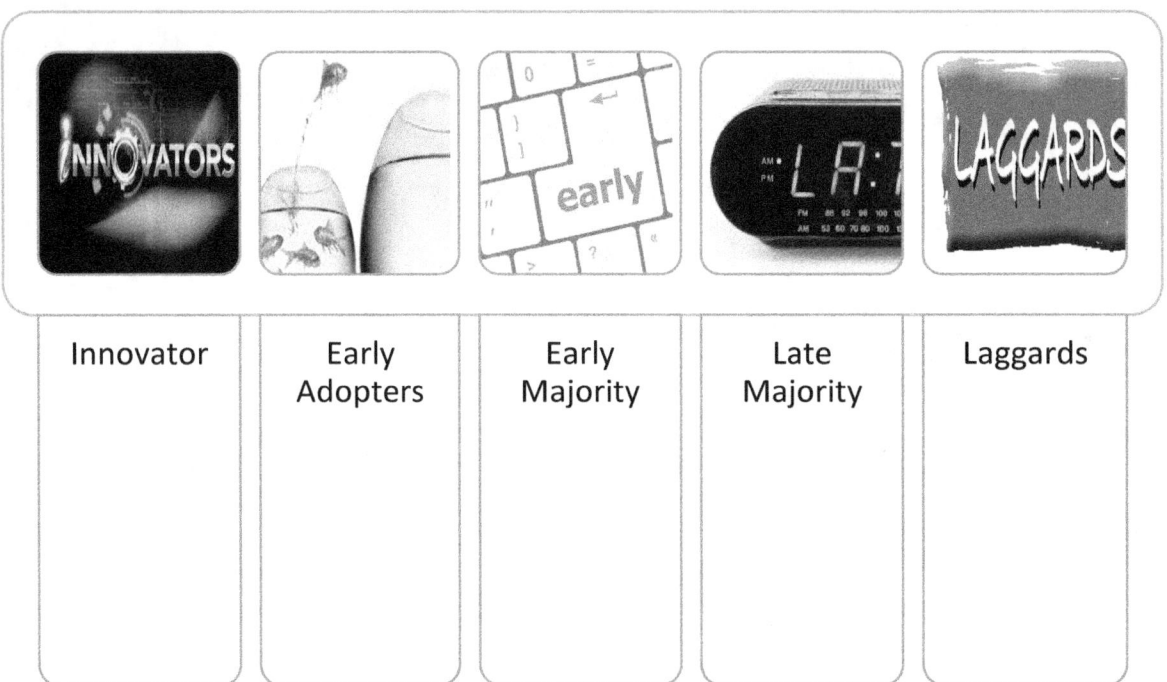

Innovator	Early Adopters	Early Majority	Late Majority	Laggards

WB Block 2: Cultivate the Mind

The questions below reflect some of the most common areas of business concerns highlighted in this block. Answer all questions. **Discuss & Share** your answers with your cohort to provide in-depth understanding for each of your responses. Make additional notes if questions/concern aren't answered immediately, information provided in previous or later blocks may also help you get clarification.

☺ (Discussion Tag)

1.   What meaning have you drawn from the Allegory of the Cave analogy? Explain

```
┌─────────────────────────────────────────────┐
│                                               │
│                                               │
│                                               │
│                                               │
│                                               │
└─────────────────────────────────────────────┘
```

● (Quick Start Tag)

1.   Change is difficult, however the mindset must shift before the changes becomes easier.

What things would you express as needed for a shift? Explain answer, did this information help

start the evolution of your mindset?

```
┌─────────────────────────────────────────────┐
│                                               │
│                                               │
│                                               │
│                                               │
│                                               │
└─────────────────────────────────────────────┘
```

🧠 (Reflection Point Tag)

1.   Which of the Critical Mental Paradigm Shifts resonates to you most? Explain why (be specific)?

```



```

🧠 (Reflection Point Tag)

2.   How does trading time for money effect business growth & development? Explain (be specific)?

```



```

🔶 (Caution Tag)

1.   Do you grasp the differences in Traditional, Passive, and Residual revenue streams? Explain

```



```

🌀 (Challenge Tag)

1.   What traps are keeping you stuck in a worker's mindset? Once identified, what positive influences can help you get unstuck?

🔥 Block Key Points:

- Shifting the mindset, must proceed business decisions

- Trading time for money leads business in no direction

- Revenue must follow a structure

⏳ Practical Exercises:

In the four (4) ESBI quadrants what are seen as pro's or cons of each. Each quadrant's definition is in the Cultivating the Mind Block of the book for review.

Employed	Self-Employed	System Owner	Investor

WB Block 3: Entrepreneurial Analysis

The questions below reflect some of the most common areas of business concerns highlighted in this block. Answer all questions. **Discuss & Share** your answers with your cohort to provide in-depth understanding for each of your responses. Make additional notes if questions/concern aren't answered immediately, information provided in previous or later blocks may also help you get clarification.

☺ (Discussion Tag)

1.   Explain the purpose of doing a business analysis.

● (Quick Start Tag)

1.   Write down your initial needs analysis responses upon formulating an idea or product.

Expound on your answers, to further develop your idea/product.

🧠 (Reflection Point Tag)

1. When would you use a GAP Analysis? Be specific

```



```

🧠 (Reflection Point Tag)

2. How does a PEST analysis affect an idea/product? Be specific

```



```

◈ (Caution Tag)

1. Does technology augment or hinder your idea/product towards optimal success? Why?

```



```

◉ (Challenge Tag)

1. What is the biggest gap that can be addressed or solved by your idea/product/company?

```
┌─────────────────────────────────────────────┐
│                                               │
│                                               │
│                                               │
│                                               │
└─────────────────────────────────────────────┘
```

Block Key Points:

- All company's (big or small) should do a needs analysis/assessment but especially prior to conducting new business

- Understand your external and internal factors; they could save you time, money and effort.

⌛ Practical Exercises:

In the four (4) categories list some things or people (to include how) that affect your

idea/company. SWOT definitions are in Entrepreneurial Analysis Block of the book for review.

Strengths	Weaknesses	Opportunities	Threats

WB Block 4: New Venture Set-up & Venture Markets

The questions below reflect some of the most common areas of business concerns highlighted in this block. Answer all questions. **Discuss & Share** your answers with your cohort to provide in-depth understanding for each of your responses. Make additional notes if questions/concern aren't answered immediately, information provided in previous or later blocks may also help you get clarification.

☺ (Discussion Tag)

1.   What are the similarities/differences in the market types (vertical, horizontal, and two-sided)?

● (Quick Start Tag)

1.   What makes your ideas/product brand worthy? Explain answer, did the information in this chapter change your outlook on your branding strategy?

♀ (Reflection Point Tag)

1.   How do you build a business portfolio from nothing? Be specific

```
[                                                                    ]
```

♀ (Reflection Point Tag)

2.   What is the core value of your idea/product/service/business? Be specific

```
[                                                                    ]
```

◈ (Caution Tag)

1.   Every idea does not equal a successful business, what are some steps that can be followed

to increase the possibility of avoiding failure?

```
[                                                                    ]
```

☀ (Challenge Tag)

1.   Do you have a niche market? If so, what positive or negative influences can affect that market?

⟶ Block Key Points:

- Planning & Research is critical to developing ideas/products/services/business

- Setting your idea/product/service/business apart from others may be the difference between failure and success

⧗ **Practical Exercise:**

Which of the four (4) categories do you foresee your idea/product/service/business having the most (to include how) difficulty in achieving. The pitfalls of business are defined in New Venture Block of the book for review.

Service Offering	Fund Excellence	Manage Quality	Appease Customers

WB Block 5: Methodology Establishment

The questions below reflect some of the most common areas of business concerns highlighted in this block. Answer all questions. **Discuss & Share** your answers with your cohort to provide in-depth understanding for each of your responses. Make additional notes if questions/concern aren't answered immediately, information provided in previous or later blocks may also help you get clarification.

☺ (Discussion Tag)

1.   What personality color best describes you? How do you communicate in view of

product/service/business as you envision it? Explain from your core values.

```
```

☺ (Discussion Tag)

2.   How does methodology tie to market? How do explain the how the method helps the

market?

```
```

● (Quick Start Tag)

1.   What are the characteristic(s) you have that you want to be recognizable to everyone you encounter? If you have yet to learn it, explain why you need it?

```
```

♀ (Reflection Point Tag)

1.   What style of leadership is displayed through your actions? From your leadership style what personality color type of people would best follow you? Be specific

```
```

♀ (Reflection Point Tag)

2.   What alignment has occurred between your core values, your methodology and your idea/product/service/business? Be specific. If none, where must you improve immediately?

```
```

◈ (Caution Tag)

1.   Do you possess core values in your product/service/business that will cause people to reject your product/service/business before you have an opportunity to build a relationship? If yes, what needs to be adjusted?

◉ (Challenge Tag)

1.   If you're not replicating yourself/core values; do you know or have someone/something to emulate temporarily? If so, what positive influences or personality color traits do they possess that you're aware of?

Block Key Points:

- Knowing your colors and how to communicate to other colors makes a difference

- Methodology is a direct reflection of personality traits and leadership style

- Core values have to be imparted into every person then maintained by those same people

⌛ **Practical Exercises:**

In the four (4) categories of C.E.S.R list some things or people (to include how) that should be part of your methodology. Methodology terminology and definitions are in Methodology Establishment Block of the book for review.

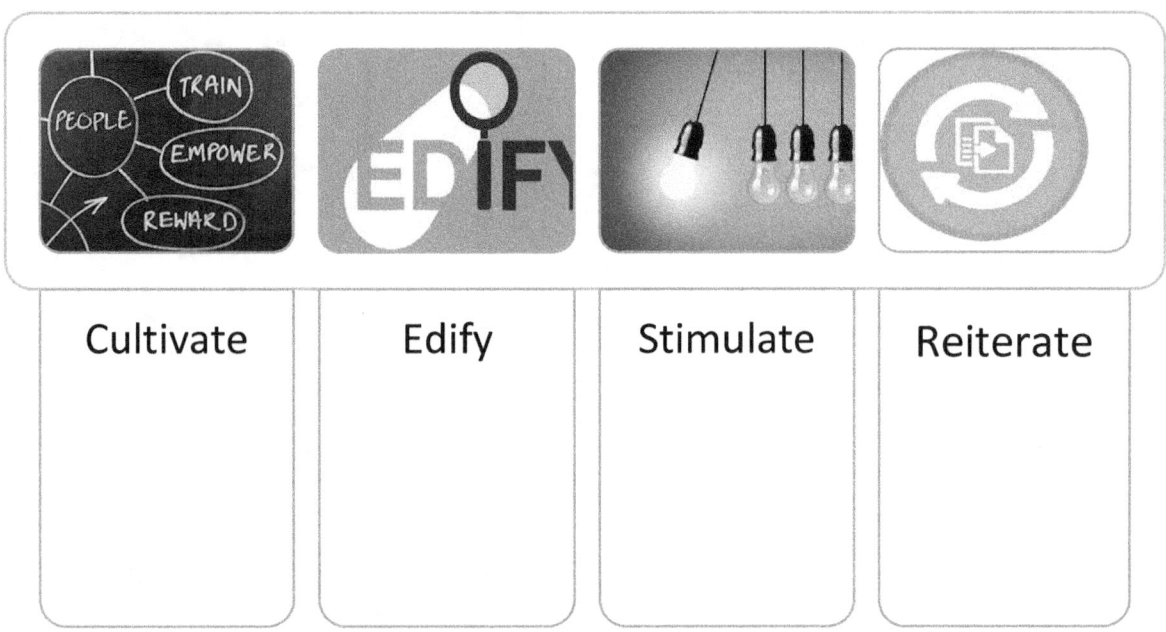

Cultivate	Edify	Stimulate	Reiterate

WB Block 6: Maintain Grow Evolve & Speed of Business

The questions below reflect some of the most common areas of business concerns highlighted in this block. Answer all questions. **Discuss & Share** your answers with your cohort to provide in-depth understanding for each of your responses. Make additional notes if questions/concern aren't answered immediately, information provided in previous or later blocks may also help you get clarification.

☺ (Discussion Tag)

1.   How can marketing analytics affect your positioning for growth? Explain from the

context of company core values.

● (Quick Start Tag)

1.   Is technology integrated into delivering your product/service? Explain answer, did this

information change the attitude towards business evolution?

• (Quick Start Tag)

2.   In the three (3) categories (workforce, organization, culture) list some things moving

slower, that is or will affect your potential growth (to include how).

```
```

♀ (Reflection Point Tag)

1.   Does your initial brand still reflect the evolution of the vision of your

product/service/business like you desire it too? Is rebranding needed, be specific?

```
```

♀ (Reflection Point Tag)

2.   What trends in business does your product/service/business generate? Be specific

```
```

```



```

◈ (Caution Tag)

1.	If the cost of change outweighs the price of potential failure by standing still; will you stay or move? Why?

```



```

◈ (Caution Tag)

2.	Staying ahead of trends can be tiresome but being behind them are detrimental to business growth? How does trends affect your product/service/business?

```



```

◉ (Challenge Tag)

1.   Does your current service/business culture move your product/service/business forward?

If not, what negative factors are standing in your path?

Block Key Points:

- Businesses need to reflect the current culture without comprising original identity

- A slow controlled growth & evolution plan is no longer ideal

- Speed and Quality by your workforce do not have to be enemies

- Trends come in ebbs and flows plan outside of them but within the speed of business

- Developing adjacencies could minimize your cost and maximize your profit margins

⧗ **Practical Exercises:**

In the five (5) categories list some of the problems that arise in the different stages of business development that have/will affect your potential growth (to include why).

Existence	Survival	Success	Take-Off	Maturity

WB Block 7: Thinking Global Acting Local

The questions below reflect some of the most common areas of business concerns highlighted in this block. Answer all questions. **Discuss & Share** your answers with your cohort to provide in-depth understanding for each of your responses. Make additional notes if questions/concern aren't answered immediately, information provided in previous or later chapters may also help with clarification.

☺ (Discussion Tag)

1.   How does thinking global but acting local tie into to knowing your market and your

company's core concept that we discussed back in Blocks 4, 5 & 6?

● (Quick Start Tag)

1.   If you're not considering globalization what steps should you be taking to achieve

mastery of localization? Explain answer, did this information change the approach towards

expansion?

👤 (Reflection Point Tag)

1.   Is your product/service/business growing faster than your local market? In what way, be detailed & specific

>

👤 (Reflection Point Tag)

2.   What is the primary industry your interest falls into? Is your primary industry expanding or contracting because of external factor like technology, demand or globalization?

>

◈ (Caution Tag)

1.   Do not expand to fast or to slow for your market base, how do you determine that point? Why is this concept important?

```



```

☮ (Challenge Tag)

1.   Is your product/service/business reaching its optimal business level currently? If not,

what can be changed immediately to progress to next level?

```



```

☞ Block Key Points:

- Local customers/supporters are generating loyalty in today's business climate

- Global is the current buzz of the business world but is it irrational to not focus your

    business's success on local support

⌛ Practical Exercises:

In the four (4) categories list some things that may improve your opportunity to achieve that level of business. Business level definitions are in Think Global Act Local Block of the book for review.

WB Block 8: $^e21^{st}$ Century Exit Exercise

The questions below reflect some of the most common areas of business concerns highlighted in this block. Answer all questions. **Discuss & Share** your answers with your cohort to provide in-depth understanding for each of your responses. Make additional notes if questions/concerns aren't answered immediately, information provided in previous blocks may also help you get clarification.

☺ (Discussion Tag)

1. What value have you concluded from the Launch Party to using this as a marketing tool?

```

```

● (Quick Start Tag)

1.   Are you capable to conducting a launch party within the next seven (7) days? If you're not what tools or training would you consider helpful?

```

```

♀ (Reflection Point Tag)

1.   Is the product & service critical to this business or is people critical to this type of

business?

```
┌─────────────────────────────────────────────────────────────┐
│                                                               │
│                                                               │
│                                                               │
│                                                               │
└─────────────────────────────────────────────────────────────┘
```

♀ (Reflection Point Tag)

2.   What does the potential fun freedom and fulfillment mean to you?

```
┌─────────────────────────────────────────────────────────────┐
│                                                               │
│                                                               │
│                                                               │
│                                                               │
└─────────────────────────────────────────────────────────────┘
```

◉ (Challenge Tag)

1.   Create a bucket list (your favorite or wish to go) of all the places, things, or events you

thought were out of your reach before? If can't think of any, start with someone else's list to

open your thinking?

Block Key Points:

- Networking is critical to being successful in this industry

- Working a JOB doesn't always provide fun freedom and fulfillment

- The business world is being disrupted without any publicity

- IF you're this point you have said yes to the best decision of your life

I SAID YES

⧗ Practical Exercises:

In the four (4) categories list some names of individuals/couples that you may enjoying doing these things in the company of.

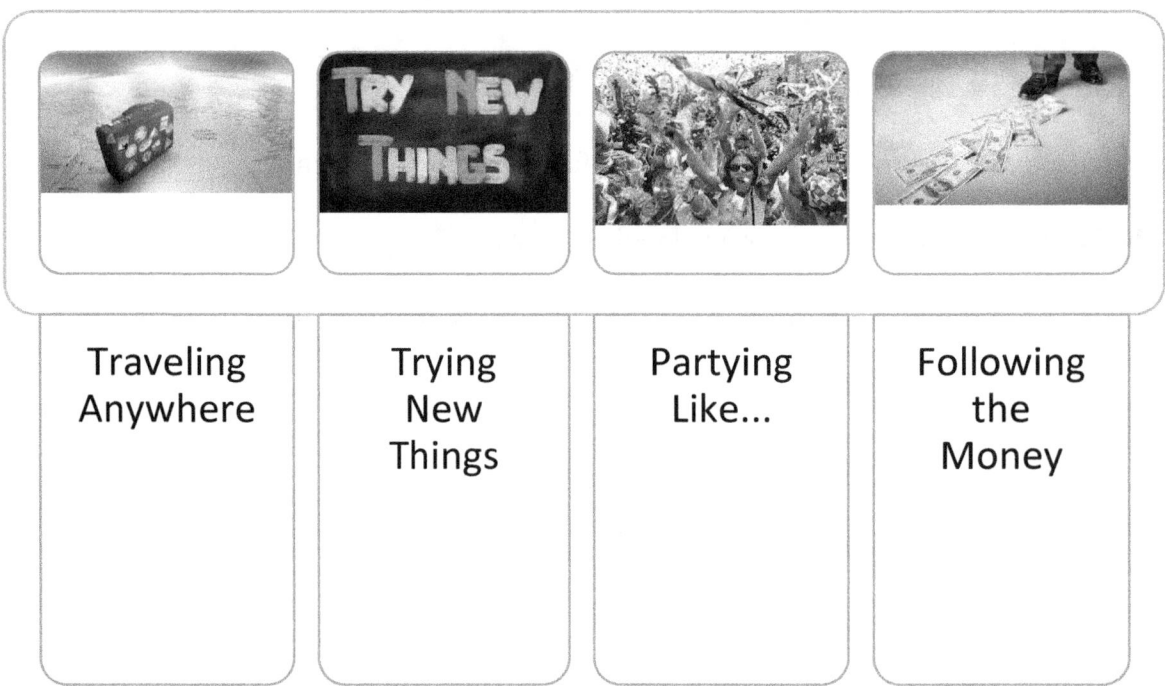

Traveling Anywhere	Trying New Things	Partying Like...	Following the Money